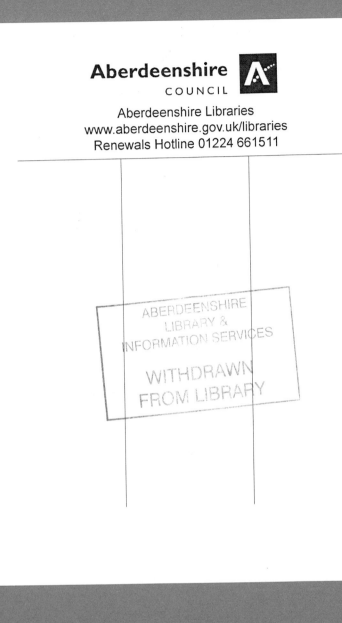

Aberdeenshire

COUNCIL

Aberdeenshire Libraries
www.aberdeenshire.gov.uk/libraries
Renewals Hotline 01224 661511

ABERDEENSHIRE
LIBRARY &
INFORMATION SERVICES

WITHDRAWN
FROM LIBRARY

D0409377

ANCIENT GREECE

Philip Steele

KINGFISHER

ABERDEENSHIRE
LIBRARY & INFO SERV

3069408	
Bertrams	12/03/2012
J938	£10.99

KINGFISHER

First published 2011 by Kingfisher
an imprint of Macmillan Children's Books
a division of Macmillan Publishers Limited
20 New Wharf Road, London N1 9RR
Basingstoke and Oxford
Associated companies throughout the world
www.panmacmillan.com

Consultant: Dr Hugh Bowden, King's College London

Illustrations by: Thomas Bayley, Peter Bull Art Studio, Gary Hanna (www.the-art-agency.co.uk),
Roger Stewart, Steve Stone (represented by Artist Partners Ltd), Steve Weston (Linden Artists)

ISBN 978-0-7534-3070-5

Copyright © Macmillan Children's Books 2011

All rights reserved. No part of this publication may be reproduced, stored
in or introduced into a retrieval system, or transmitted, in any form or by any means
(electronic, mechanical, photocopying, recording or otherwise), without the prior written
permission of the publisher. Any person who does any unauthorized act in relation to this
publication may be liable to criminal prosecution and civil claims for damages.

5 7 9 8 6
5TR/1111/UG/WKT/140MA

A CIP catalogue record for this book is available from the British Library.

Printed in China

This book is sold subject to the condition that it shall not, by way
of trade or otherwise, be lent, resold, hired out, or otherwise circulated
without the publisher's prior consent in any form of binding or cover
other than that in which it is published and without a similar condition
including this condition being imposed on the subsequent purchaser.

Note to readers: The website addresses listed in this book are correct at the time of publishing.
However, due to the ever-changing nature of the internet, website addresses and content can change.
Websites can contain links that are unsuitable for children. The publisher cannot be held responsible for
changes in website addresses or content, or for information obtained through third-party websites.
We strongly advise that internet searches should be supervised by an adult.

**The Publisher would like to thank the following for permission to reproduce their material. Every care has been taken to trace copyright holders.
However, if there have been unintentional omissions or failure to trace copyright holders, we apologise and will, if informed, endeavour to make
corrections in any future edition. (t = top, b = bottom, c = centre, r = right, l = left):**

Front cover: tl Alamy/The Art Gallery Collection; tr Getty/Digital Vision; c Steve Stone; bl Shutterstock/Nick Paviakis; br Shutterstock/Paul Picone; back cover: Shutterstock/Tramont_ana; and inside pages
4tl Photolibrary/Flirt Collection; 4br Photolibrary/Robert Harding; 5b Shutterstock/markrhiggins; 6cl Art Archive (AA)/Heraklion Archaeological Museum, Crete; 6br AA/Bibliothèque des Arts Decoratif;
7tr AKG/Heraklion Archaeological Museum, Crete; 8tc AA/National Archaeological Museum, Athens/Dagli Orti; 8tr AA/National Archaeological Museum, Athens/Dagli Orti; 9tl AA/National Archaeological
Museum, Athens/Dagli Orti; 9tr AA/National Archaeological Museum, Athens/Dagli Orti; 9br AA/National Archaeological Museum, Athens/Dagli Orti; 10bl AA/National Archaeological Museum, Athens/Dagli
Orti; 11tl AKG/Warner Bros/Alex Bailey; 11tr With the kind permission of the Trustees of the British Museum; 12tr AKG/British Museum; 15bl AKG/SMPK Antiquities Museum; 16tl AKG/Archives CDA/Guillo;
16bl iStockphoto; 17bc AKG/Erich Lessing; 18cl AKG/Erich Lessing; 18bl AKG/Narodowe Museum, Warsaw; 19t AA/Archaeological Museum, Sparta/Gianni Dagli Orti; 21tl Corbis/Gianni Dagli Orti; 22c
Shutterstock/James M House; 22–23 Shutterstock/Maximmal; 23tl AKG/Erich Lessing; 23cr AA/Agora Museum, Athens/Gianni Dagli Orti; 23cl With the kind permission of the Trustees of the British Museum;
23br Getty/Time & Life Pictures; 23r Shutterstock/Alice; 24bl AKG/Musée du Louvre; 26–27 Art Archive/Bibliothèque des Arts Decoratifs, Paris/Dagli Orti; 26tr AA/Musée du Louvre/Dagli Orti; 26cl AKG/
Musée du Louvre; 27 iStockphoto; 28tl AA/Superstock; 28bc AA/Kanellopoulos Museum, Athens/Dagli Orti; 28r AKG/Kunsthistorisches Museum, Vienna; 29l Shutterstock/Denis Kornilov; 29tr With the
kind permission of the Trustees of the British Museum; 29cc AA/Agora Museum, Athens/Dagli Orti; 29cr AA/Soprintendenza Archaeologica, Salerno/Dagli Orti; 30tl Shutterstock/Panos Karapanagiotis;
30rc Shutterstock/RoxyFer; 30bl AKG/Erich Lessing; 30bc AA/Musée du Louvre; 30br AA/Musée du Louvre; 31tl Shutterstock/Oleg Seleznev; 31r Shutterstock/bumihills; 31bl Bridgeman Art Library/Ancient
Art & Architecture; 32tr AA/Kanellopoulos Museum, Athens/Dagli Orti; 32cl AA/Museo Nazionale Terme, Rome/Gianni Dagli Orti; 33tr AA/Museo di Villa Giulia, Rome/Gianni Dagli Orti; 33cr Shutterstock/
Evangelos; 34tl AA/Archaeological Museum, Istanbul/ Dagli Orti; 34tr AKG/Erich Lessing; 35tl AKG/Erich Lessing; 36br PA/AP; 37tl AKG/British Library; 37tr AA/Museo Nazionale Romano, Rome/Dagli Orti;
37cl AA/National Archaeological Museum, Athens/Gianni Dagli Orti; 37br AKG/North Wind Archives; 38–39 AA/ Musée Archéologique, Naples/Alfredo Dagli Orti; 38br Kobal/Warner Bros/Jaap Buitendijk;
39tr AKG/Bildarchiv Steffens; 40bl AKG/Erich Lessing; 41cr Kingfisher/Steve Weston; 41br Getty/Lonely Planet; 42tl Marie-Lan Nguy; 42b Photolibrary/Waterframe; 43tl AKG/Nimatallah; 43cr Album/Oronoz;
43br PA/AP; 48tl AA/Museo Nazionale Reggio, Calabria/Dagli Orti; 48cl Photolibrary/P Narayan; 48cr Kobal/Warner Bros/Jaap Buitendijk; 48bl Shutterstock/Jozef Sedmak.

CONTENTS

CIVILIZATION – a society that has developed government, laws, arts, science and technology

ILLYRIA

MACEDONIA

gold coin of Philip II of Macedon showing the hero Heracles

THRACE

About 80 per cent of the Greek mainland is taken up by mountains and hills.

EPIRUS

CHALCIDICE

AEGEAN SEA

Mount Olympus, home of the gods

MOUNT OLYMPUS

CORFU

THESSALY

PINDUS MOUNTAINS

GREECE CYNOSCEPHALAE •

AETOLIA

THERMOPYLAE •

LOCRIS DELPHI •

PHOCIS
• ORCHOMENUS

EUBOEA
• CHALCIS
• ERETRIA

BOEOTIA
• THEBES
• PLATAEA

ATTICA • MARATHON
• ATHENS

ACHAEA

Delphi, a major religious site

MEGARA • SALAMIS

PIRAEUS

• ELIS

CORINTH •
NEMEA •
MYCENAE •
ARGOS • • TIRYNS • EPIDAURUS

Parthenon, a temple that overlooks the city of Athens, the most powerful state in Greece, c. 400s BCE

OLYMPIA
•

ANCIENT CIVILIZATIONS

Ruined cities, temples and theatres can still be seen in Greece. Most date from the great age of the Greek city-states, between the 700s and 300s BCE. The civilizations that flourished in Greece between 5,000 and 2,300 years ago still affect the way we see the world today.

PELOPONNESE

MESSENIA

• SPARTA

LACONIA

statue of Zeus at Olympia, c. 432BCE

• PYLOS

Sparta, a military state

IONIAN SEA

VOYAGE TO GREECE

Greece can be visited by ship, crossing the dark-blue waters of the Aegean or Ionian seas. Island after island appears on the horizon. Beyond them lies the Greek mainland, where mountains and rocky shores surround plains and groves of olive trees. The climate is hot and dry in summer, but mild and moist in winter. In ancient times this beautiful, sunny land was called Hellas.

ACROSS THE WAVES

These fish and dolphins were painted at the palace of Knossos on the island of Crete more than 3,500 years ago. Greece is a land of coasts and islands. Its seas were sailed by fishermen, merchants, pirates and warriors.

MEDITERRANEAN SEA

> Earthquakes are common in Greece. They were said to be the work of the god Poseidon (see page 14).

BLACK SEA

BYZANTIUM •

Bosphorus Strait divides
Europe from Asia

SEA OF MARMARA

PHRYGIA

• TROY

*Greek soldiers were said
to have hidden inside a
wooden horse to gain
access to the city of Troy*

LESBOS   MYSIA

ASIA MINOR

• PHOCAEA

CHIOS   • SMYRNA   LYDIA

AEGEAN SEA

SAMOS   • EPHESUS

• PRIENE

DELOS

CYCLADES   IONIA   CARIA

NAXOS

• HALICARNASSUS

LYCIA

THERA
(SANTORINI)

*massive volcanic
eruption on
Santorini,
c. 1600BCE*

SEA OF CRETE

*Minoan palace
of Knossos,
c. 1700–1350BCE*

KNOSSOS

CRETE

RHODES

LANDS OF THE GREEKS

The Greek mainland forms part of the Balkan peninsula, in southern Europe. Its ragged coastline breaks up into headlands, inlets and chains of islands. These divide the eastern Mediterranean into a number of smaller seas, straits and gulfs. In ancient times, Greeks also settled along the coasts of Asia Minor, or Anatolia (in modern Turkey).

KEY

religious place

site of a battle

"FUTURE AGES WILL WONDER
AT US, AS THE PRESENT AGE
WONDERS AT US NOW."

words of the Athenian leader Pericles
as reported by the historian Thucydides (c. 460–395BCE)

⊖ THE GREEK SPIRIT

For most of its history, Greece was not united as a single nation. Instead, it was made up of rival cities and small city-states. Sometimes these joined forces, but often they fought against each other. Even so, throughout most of their history, all Greeks shared similar ways of life, the same language, view of the world and religious practices.

Greek horsemen ride through Athens

www.ancientgreece.co.uk/time/explore/exp_set.html

PEOPLE OF THE PALACE

Crete is the largest island in Greece. It has high mountains and is surrounded by sparkling, blue sea. It was here that Europe's first great civilization grew, between about 2700 and 1420BCE. Its people worked with metals and traded with the rest of Europe, Egypt and Asia. The legendary ruler of Crete was called Minos, so this civilization is often called 'Minoan'.

THE BULLS OF KNOSSOS

It was daring, death-defying and acrobatic! Young men, and probably young women, too, would vault over the horns of a bull and perform somersaults. Bulls were sacred in Crete, so this sport was probably part of a religious ritual, watched by the royal court at Knossos.

PRINCE OF THE LILIES

Beautiful wall paintings have been found at Knossos, the site of a splendid palace. They show lords and ladies, flowers, birds and dolphins. Fine Minoan paintings have also been found on the nearby island of Thera (Santorini), which was destroyed by a massive volcanic eruption about 3,600 years ago.

CRETE'S DARK SECRET

Ancient myths tell of a savage monster called the Minotaur, who was half-man and half-bull. He was imprisoned in the Labyrinth, a maze built by a cunning engineer named Daedalus. Eventually, the hero Theseus, who founded the city of Athens, discovered a way through the maze and killed the monster (right).

An acrobat waits to catch the bull-leaper.

> The eruption of Thera may have triggered a tsunami, a huge ocean wave, that devastated the coast of Crete.

Vaults and somersaults require perfect timing.

THE DOUBLE AXE

Goddesses were more significant than gods in Minoan religion. They are sometimes shown with an axe called a *labrys*, which may have been used to sacrifice bulls. Small, ornamental axes were used as amulets or charms.

The *labrys* had twin blades.

Cretan bulls have long, sharp horns.

www.britannica.com/EBchecked/topic/384401/Minoan-civilization

CITADEL – a stronghold or fortress defending a settlement or city

LORDS OF THE CITADEL

On rocks above the plains of mainland Greece, royal halls and new settlements began to appear. They were the homes of kings, queens and warrior bands. Fortified citadels with strong stone walls have been discovered at Tiryns, Thebes, Pylos, Athens, Orchomenus and Mycenae. We call this civilization 'Mycenaean'. From about 1600BCE, the Mycenaeans became ever more powerful. They eventually conquered Minoan Crete.

bronze dagger blades inlaid with gold, from Mycenae, 1500s BCE

gold-handled dagger from Pylos, 1500s BCE

THE WARRIORS

Mycenaean warriors fought with swords, daggers and long spears. They wore bronze armour and bore large shields covered in ox hide. Chariots carried them to battle.

two lionesses carved in stone above the gate

> A myth claimed that the walls of Mycenae and Tiryns were built by one-eyed giants, known as the Cyclopes.

A CUP FOR A KING

The Mycenaeans often used Minoan goldsmiths. This gold cup features a picture of a bull. It was found at Vapheio, near Sparta in southern Greece, and was made between 1500 and 1400BCE.

THROUGH THE LION GATE

The citadel of Mycenae overlooked the Argive plain, 90km to the west of Athens. Its 900m-long walls were made of huge, strong stone blocks, some of them weighing as much as 12 tonnes. The walls would have been up to 12m high and 7m thick. The Lion Gate was the entrance to the palace within the walls. A town spread across the lower slopes, outside the fortification.

A NOBLE WOMAN

This lady appears on a wall painting from Mycenae. She dates from the 1200s BCE and wears rich clothes and jewellery. The Mycenaean nobles were wealthy, and enjoyed perfumes, fine pottery, linen and woollen textiles, and tiled floors.

main gates were defended by extended walls called bastions

www.namuseum.gr/collections/prehistorical/mycenian-en.html

MASK OF GOLD

This magnificent gold mask was placed over the face of a man who was buried in the graves at Mycenae. It was discovered in 1876 by a great German archaeologist called Heinrich Schliemann. He thought he had found the remains of a legendary Greek king called Agamemnon, but the mask dates from 1550 to 1500BCE, centuries before the time when Agamemnon was believed to have ruled.

so-called Mask of Agamemnon

Battle chariots are pulled by two horses.

The Trojan citadel is set on fire by the enemy.

Long, bronze swords are used for hand-to-hand fighting.

A Mycenaean champion engages in combat.

COLLAPSE OF THE PALACES

The Mycenaean age came to an end around 1200BCE when the great palaces were destroyed. Clay tablets, written in a script called Linear B, survive from some of the palaces and tell us about the Mycenaeans and their society.

WAR WITH TROY

Mycenaean warriors sailed to attack islands and coasts around the Aegean sea. They wore helmets made of boars' tusks, and fought fiercely with bronze weapons. They attacked fortified cities such as Troy, in what is now Turkey. For hundreds of years Greeks liked to tell exciting tales about their battles with Troy. These may have been based on many different conflicts, or possibly on one great 'Trojan War' in the 1190s and 1180s BCE.

> Greeks told of how the Trojan War started when Helen, a beautiful queen, was carried off by Paris, prince of Troy.

WOODEN HORSE

This scene is from the film *Troy* (2004), which is based on a story from the *Iliad* (see panel, right). A huge wooden horse is shown being hauled into the Trojan citadel. Greek soldiers were hiding inside the horse. They tricked the Trojans into defeat.

HOMER'S HEROES

Deadly combat, treachery, bravery, love and fate all play a part in one of the most famous tales ever told, the *Iliad*. Its stirring poetry imagines a time late in the Trojan War and describes, in detail, great battles of Greek and Trojan warriors. The *Iliad* was probably written soon after 700BCE, but it was based on songs handed down by generations of skilled poets. Did these songs include memories that reached back to Mycenaean times?

the *Iliad*'s Greek hero, Achilles (left), in battle

www.bbc.co.uk/schools/troy

GREEKS VERSUS TROJANS

For many years, scholars believed that accounts of the Trojan War were no more than stories. Then, between 1871 and 1890, the German archaeologist Heinrich Schliemann discovered the remains of the city of Troy near Hisarlik in Turkey. We now know that this site was occupied over thousands of years – and shows evidence of destruction in about 1180BCE.

"HECTOR LEAPT TO THE GROUND FROM HIS CHARIOT FULLY ARMED... DRIVING HIS FIGHTERS INTO BATTLE."

Homer
earliest Greek poet, from the Iliad (c. 680BCE)

The Myceneans' long spears protect the front rank. They are not thrown.

COLONIST – someone who settles in another land

⊜ THE VOYAGES OF ODYSSEUS

What happened after the Trojan War? Homer's *Odyssey* tells the story of a warrior king called Odysseus, whose journey home to Ithaca takes ten long years. This is an exciting tale about gods, goddesses, monsters and bird-women called Sirens, who lure sailors to death with their singing. We hear of shipwrecks, magic and revenge. At the time these stories were written, after 700BCE, many Greeks were already seafaring far from home.

Odysseus and the Sirens

Greek islands

Colonists sail in search of new lands.

SEAS AND CITIES

The citadels of the Mycenaeans lay in ruins after centuries of war. In their place new communities appeared. Iron, which was harder and tougher than bronze, was being hammered into weapons and tools. Greece became a patchwork of small states. These were based on islands, or on a single city and its surrounding land. Each city-state (called a *polis*) was independent. Famous city-states included Athens, Sparta, Thebes and Corinth.

CARGOES AND TRADE

Greek merchants, known as *emporoi*, shipped wheat, timber, marble, silver and pottery. Wine and olive oil were transported in pottery jars called *amphorae*.

amphorae

Sailors carry cargo on board.

> Colonists took fire from the mother city to start their first fire in the new colony.

THE WIDER WORLD

Many Greek city-states were hemmed in by mountains or rocky coasts with poor soil for farming. Groups of settlers went out in search of better land to build new communities. These overseas colonies were independent, but kept strong links with their 'mother city' (or *metropolis*). Greeks settled around the Black Sea, in Asia Minor, North Africa, Italy, France and Spain. Some of Europe's best known cities, including Naples in Italy and Marseille in France, were Greek colonies.

www.ancientgreece.co.uk/geography/home_set.html

A GREEK CITY
This Greek city is built by the coast, on a steep hillside. It has a busy harbour for fishing boats and merchant ships. A road leads from the marketplace and the houses to a high rock, where there is a temple built of marble.

ACROSS THE WAVES
This wooden merchant ship uses oars as well as a large, square sail. It is steered by one man with a long side oar near the stern.

naukleros or ship-owner

ORACLE – a shrine where people could consult the gods about the future

Hephaestus
god of fire, blacksmiths and forges

Aphrodite
goddess of love and beauty, whose symbol was a dove

Dionysus
god of wine and drama, who was worshipped at wild festivals

Ares
god of war and a bloodthirsty warrior, whose father was Zeus

Hera
wife of Zeus and queen of the gods, who was also the goddess of marriage

Poseidon
god of the sea, earthquakes and horses, often shown holding a trident

GODS OF OLYMPUS

Early Greek stories told how the universe was created from chaos. Out of this the first gods and goddesses came into being, representing the earth, the sea, the sky, and night and day. The Greeks had tales about many other gods as well. These represented human feelings such as love, forces of nature such as earthquakes, or human activities such as farming or fighting. Stories of giants, monsters, spirits and heroes were also told.

peaks of Mount Olympus

POWER AND FATE

The most important gods and goddesses were said to live at the snowy summit of Greece's highest mountain, Olympus. They were ruled by Zeus, god of the sky, and were like humans, forever quarrelling amongst themselves. The gods and goddesses controlled the fate of human beings – they punished them, rewarded them, bewitched them and sometimes even fell in love with them.

"THEN WE WENT TO THE GOD'S PRECINCT, AND THERE ON THE ALTAR OUR CAKES AND OFFERINGS WERE DEDICATED, FOOD FOR HEPHAESTUS' FLAME."

Aristophanes (c. 448–388BCE)
Greek poet, from his play Wealth (c. 388BCE)

> One myth tells that Athena was so jealous of Arachne the weaver's skills that she turned her into a spider.

http://library.thinkquest.org/J002356F/godlibrary.htm

Artemis
moon goddess and a huntress with a bow and arrow

Hermes
messenger of the gods, who was worshipped by businessmen – and thieves!

Athena
patron goddess of Athens, victorious in battle and worshipped for her wisdom

Demeter
mother goddess representing fertility, farming and the seasons

Apollo
god of light, who was also linked with music, poetry and archery

Zeus
king of the gods, god of the sky, and the commander of thunder and lightning

⊖ THE ORACLE AT DELPHI

Delphi was a religious site on the slopes of Mount Parnassus. It was sacred to Apollo, who killed Python, a snake goddess who guarded the earth. Delphi was famous for its oracle. A priestess would go into a trance and speak the words of Apollo. Rulers and the famous would visit Delphi for guidance about their futures.

consulting the oracle (priestess is seated on the left)

TO THE TEMPLE

Greeks made offerings to the gods at their temples. Each year there would be a public procession to the temple in honour of a god or goddess, bringing an animal such as a sheep for sacrifice. At least one priest would have accompanied the procession on its journey.

TO VICTORY

Warriors and chariots decorate the rim of this bronze krater, a vase used for mixing wine and water. It was made in Laconia around 530BCE, but found far away in France. Bronze work was a key export from Laconia.

design celebrating the victory of warriors

shield (hoplon) of bronze, wood and leather

stabbing spear, 2m to 3m long

helmet with horsehair crest

THE SNARLING FOX

A Spartan boy once stole a fox. He hid it beneath his cloak. When challenged, he refused to own up, even though the fox was gnawing and biting. He died of his wounds. The Spartans saw no shame in stealing, only in being found out.

FIGHTING FIT

In Sparta, the physically weak might be killed at birth. From an early age, Spartan boys were trained in physical exercise, wrestling and combat. Cowards ('tremblers') were despised.

learning to wrestle

> HOPLITE - an armed foot soldier in ancient Greece

SHIELDS OF SPARTA

Who needs stone walls around their city if they have the bravest warriors? That was the proud boast of the city-state of Sparta. The Spartans were certainly the toughest fighters in Greece. They conquered the regions of Laconia and Messenia in the south by about 550BCE and forced the local people to work for them as labourers called 'helots'. This left the Spartans free – to train for war.

bronze greave (shin guard) to protect lower leg

THE RED CLOAKS

At the age of seven, Spartan boys were taken from their parents and sent to live in a barracks with others of the same age. The discipline was very harsh. From the age of 20, a male could wear the famous red cloak of a Spartan warrior, or hoplite (literally meaning 'shield-bearer'). The hoplite could be called up to fight at any time until he reached the age of 60. Their armour was expensive and each hoplite had to buy his own. Dead hoplites were carried from the battlefield on their shields.

SPARTAN GIRLS

Girls in Sparta were taught to race and wrestle. Most Greeks were shocked by this. Elsewhere, young women were expected to stay inside their house, spin and weave wool, and give birth to children.

⟩ The Spartans were ruled not by one king, but by two at the same time.

THE IMMORTALS

Xerxes' Persian army, perhaps 250,000 strong, was led by elite troops (left), known as the Immortals. As the Spartan King Leonidas marched north, he gained the support of only a few thousand hoplites from other Greek states. No large army followed after him.

TO THERMOPYLAE

By the summer of 480BCE, the Persians were approaching Thermopylae, a narrow pass between the seashore and mountains in central Greece. An advance party of 300 Spartan hoplites rushed north. Their job seemed impossible – to hold back or delay the Persian advance.

Greek hoplite attacking Persian cavalry

Wave after wave of Persians attack the Greek line.

> EMPIRE - *many different lands brought together under a single ruler*

FIGHTING IN THE SHADE

The Spartans showed no fear. A local man warned that the Persians had so many archers that their arrows would block the sun. A hoplite called Dieneces laughed and said, "Good! Then we'll be fighting in the shade!" Throughout the first day of battle, wave after wave of Persian troops, even Immortals, fell to the Spartan spears. At the end of the second day, Leonidas still held the pass, even though no Greek reinforcements had arrived.

The Spartans hold the pass until the third day.

bust of King Leonidas I of Sparta, who died in 480BCE

THE LAST STAND

In the end, the Persians bribed a local Greek to show them a secret path through the mountains. On the third day, Leonidas was attacked by Persians from all sides. Most other troops went home, but some Greek allies stayed to fight. It took the Greeks another year to finally beat off the Persians, on another battlefield – Plataea.

BATTLE IN THE PASS

About 2,500 years ago, Persia ruled the world's biggest empire. It stretched from Egypt to India and included Greek colonies in Asia Minor. These eastern Greeks revolted in 499BCE, starting a war. A Persian invasion of the Greek mainland failed in 490BCE, but in 481BCE, a new Persian king called Xerxes decided to seek revenge. He assembled a vast army and fleet. Its mission was the conquest of all Greece, by land and sea.

"GO, STRANGER, AND TELL THEM IN SPARTA THAT WE LIE HERE, OBEDIENT TO THEIR COMMANDS."

Simonides (c. 556–468BCE)
Greek poet, his lines in memory of the Spartans who died at Thermopylae

> We still use the word 'laconic' (meaning Spartan) to describe someone who uses few words.

SHIPS AT WAR

Two long sweeps (steering oars) are operated by a helmsman at the stern.

TRIREME – a warship with three banks of oars

After 490BCE, the city-state of Athens built a large navy. Soon it ruled the waves. Hundreds of warships could dock at Piraeus, the city's seaport. The fastest type of ship was the trireme, which used oar power to ram and sink the enemy. It had a mast with a single, square sail, but in battle the deck was stripped bare for action.

A double flute called an aulos is blown to help the oarsmen keep time. The crew sing as they row into battle.

THREE BANKS OF OARS

Trireme (in Greek *trieres*) means a 'three-oar' ship. The rowers were seated on staggered benches at three levels. Each oar was 4m to 4.2m in length.

> The Delphic oracle predicted Athens would be saved by its 'wooden walls'. The Athenians said that this meant its ships.

SEND IN THE MARINES

On the twin runways of the deck there was a group of up to 20 marines, or *epibatai*, including archers and armed hoplites for boarding enemy ships. The working crew of sailors numbered about 15.

MUSCLE POWER

Each ship needed 170 rowers, one to each oar. They were not slaves, but professional sailors, mostly from poorer households. The top speed was about 8 knots (15km/h).

BATTLE AT SALAMIS

After the battle of Thermopylae in 480BCE, the Persians were poised to conquer Greece. Athens was in flames. However, 21 western Greek city-states raised a fleet of 378 ships. The huge Persian fleet included Phoenicians, Egyptians and eastern Greeks, all from lands ruled by Persia. The western Greeks trapped the enemy in a channel by the island of Salamis. The battle lasted eight hours and 200 Persian ships were destroyed.

http://h2g2.com/dna/h2g2/A3114748

A trireme fatally rams an enemy ship so that it is holed at the waterline. Its rowers are thrown into the sea on impact.

Persian fleet

Athenian ships

"IMMEDIATELY SHIP STRUCK INTO SHIP ITS BRONZE-TIPPED PROW."
Aeschylus (c. 525–456BCE)
Greek dramatist, who served at Salamis, describes the battle in his play The Persians *(472BCE)*

The ram is a strong timber beam plated with bronze. It smashes into enemy ships.

DEMOCRACY – a state governed by its citizens or by their representatives

ATHENS IN ITS GLORY

During the 400s BCE, Athens experienced a golden age. Its large fleet of warships made it the most powerful of the Greek city-states. Athens benefited from the Attica region's rich silver mines and grew wealthy through trade. The city became an exciting centre of discussion and new ideas, of philosophy, politics, drama, writing, sculpture, architecture and fine craft skills.

THE GODDESS CITY

Athens was built around a high, rocky stronghold, or Acropolis. On top of this was the Parthenon, a great temple to the goddess Athena, who protected the city. It housed a statue of ivory and gold, almost 13m high. The city spread out below, a sea of tiled roofs and white walls. There were houses and courtyards, law courts and market halls. About 250,000 people may have lived in Athens and the surrounding region.

The Parthenon was a temple made from white marble. This rich stone displayed the wealth of the city.

It was said that Athena created the olive tree as a gift for the city of Athens.

www.bbc.co.uk/schools/primaryhistory/ancient_greeks/athens

SILVER OWL

Athenians minted coins of silver. This one shows an owl, the emblem of Athena, the goddess of wisdom. Owl coins were traded for goods across the ancient world.

⊜ PEOPLE POWER

Our word 'politics' comes from *polis*, Greek for 'city-state'. Athens was the first state to attempt to be ruled by its own people. This system was called *demokratía* or democracy. All citizens could attend the assembly to make political decisions. Court cases were decided by juries of hundreds of citizens. But women and slaves were excluded from democracy.

jurors' tickets used in the *dikasterion* (law court) in Athens, in the 4th century BCE

"OUR CONSTITUTION IS NAMED A DEMOCRACY, BECAUSE IT IS IN THE HANDS NOT OF THE FEW BUT OF THE MANY."

Thucydides (c. 460–400BCE)
Athenian politician and historian, from his
History of the Peloponnesian War, Book 1 *(431BCE)*

THE AGE OF PERICLES

Pericles lived from about 495 to 429BCE. He was a great Athenian statesman, a brilliant public speaker, and a military leader who also encouraged the arts and the creation of beautiful architecture.

RIVAL POWERS

After the war with Persia, the Greek city-states formed a military alliance, called the Delian League, controlled by Athens. Its power was challenged by a Peloponnesian League, led by Sparta. From 431 to 404BCE, Greek fought against Greek, by land and sea.

DAILY LIFE

Older Greek towns grew up around a maze of streets and alleys. Later cities were better planned. Around the town you might see women with pottery jars fetching the daily water supply from street fountains or wells, slaves loading donkeys with supplies or children playing in the dust. The agora was the chief meeting place. This was where the men came to do business or talk politics, and where traders came to sell their goods.

AGORA – a district serving as the centre of public life in a Greek town

THE WOMEN'S ROOM

Women married when they were about 15 years old. They spent many hours each week spinning yarn and weaving cloth. In this room they might also play music, nurse their children or take their meals.

bedroom

bathroom

kitchen

GREEK CHILDHOOD

Many babies died at birth. Those who survived were given their name after a week or so. Athenian boys might be taught their father's trade, or go to school to learn reading, writing, sums, music and gymnastics. Girls might learn at home, studying reading, writing, music and weaving. At about 12, children were expected to give their toys to the gods, as a sign that they were grown up.

child taking toy to an altar, c. 425BCE

ENSLAVED

There may have been as many slaves as free citizens in ancient Greece. They had to work as servants, nurses, cooks, labourers or miners. Some were born into slavery or sold as slaves when children. Others had been captured in wars.

Woollen blankets, clothes and wall hangings were woven on upright looms.

women's room

slaves' quarters

INSIDE THE HOME

Most homes were built of mud bricks and plaster, and had stone foundations and tiled roofs. Windows were small with wooden shutters. Wives managed the household and spent much of their time in the women's room. They had few rights, although in Sparta they could own property. Men led more public lives. Their room was used for business meetings or for entertaining friends.

www.ancientgreece.co.uk/dailylife/challenge/cha_set.html

men's room

entrance hall

bedroom

Couches laid out for a symposium (a drinking and discussion party).

playing knucklebones

store room

courtyard

juggling

workshop

THE COURTYARD

In the courtyard, slaves might be carrying in the shopping or sweeping up. Children would be playing or having lessons under a shady olive tree. Also, cooking or eating might take place here on sunny days.

PLAYTIME

Games included juggling (above) and knucklebones, in which five small bones or stones were tossed, caught and flipped on the hand. Small children played with dolls, toy animals, wheeled carts and yo-yos.

FEEDING THE PEOPLE

SYMPOSIUM – a party for men, with eating, drinking, discussion and entertainment

Greek farmers grew olive trees and grape vines, and raised sheep, goats, pigs, geese and chickens. Fields were ploughed with oxen and hardy crops of barley – or wheat in the more fertile valleys – were harvested with sickles each July. Summers were hot and dusty. Farmers built stone terraces across their rocky land to stop the soil being blown away by wind or washed away by rain.

HUNTING AND FISHING

This picture shows a famous boar hunt from Greek mythology. The countryside offered plenty of animals for hunting, including wild boar, deer and hares. Thrushes and doves were trapped for food, and fish and octopuses were netted or speared along the coasts.

STIR IT UP

A woman uses a long ladle to stir a cauldron of stew, as it simmers over the fire. In the home, a kitchen oven was used for baking and a portable brazier was used for outdoor cooking in the courtyard (see page 25).

Symposium guests reclined as they ate and drank.

> Poorer men ate and drank cheap wine at taverns called *kapeleia* rather than host an expensive symposium.

SEAFOOD AND WINE

Breakfast in ancient Greece might have been little more than a barley cake or a plate of porridge, and lunch was a simple crust of bread, goats cheese, figs or an egg. The evening meal was more substantial, perhaps with beans, lentils, onions, chicken, sausage or seafood, pears or pomegranates. While women ate in their own rooms, wealthy men and their guests would eat in theirs. A male party, or symposium, included much drinking of wine. There might be serious discussions and arguments, or entertainments with dancing girls and drinking games.

olive oil

herbs

wheat

onions

cheese

grapes

beans

honey

fish

eggs

shellfish

figs

IN THE KITCHEN

Olive oil was stored in jars. Certain meats were often eaten as part of religious rituals, but fish could be bought at any market and was preserved by salting or drying. Wild herbs and garlic added flavour, and honey was used to sweeten cakes. Vegetables and fruit were eaten in season, making for a healthy diet.

Strong wine was mixed with water and drunk from a kylix (a wide, shallow cup).

www.my-greek-recipes.com/ancient-greek-food-recipes.html

LINEN – *a smooth, cool textile made from a plant called flax*

HAIR FASHION

Greek women had long, flowing locks. In Sparta these were tied back in a ponytail, but in Athens the hair was braided into a bun with ribbons. Later fashions tucked curled hair into bands, nets and beautiful headdresses. Wigs and hair extensions were popular.

RIBBONS AND ROBES

Most Greek clothes were beautiful, but simple. They were woven on looms at home and were usually made from high-quality wool or linen. White cloth was popular, but bold colours could also be produced using natural dyes made from plants, insects and shellfish. By the 400s BCE, expensive silks and cottons were being imported from China and India.

The tunic falls in natural folds.

THE LOOK

Mirrors were made of polished bronze. What did they reflect? Rich women used make-up such as eye-liner and blusher, and powder to make the face pale. They did not want to look like poor women, who became sunburned working in the fields.

DRAPES AND FOLDS

This woman wears a peplos tunic. She has draped an outer wrap from her shoulder pin around her hips. Outer wraps were called himatia and could also be worn to veil the head or act as a cloak.

 Face powder was made from lead and was, in fact, poisonous.

WHAT TO WEAR

Greek dress was based on a tunic design, made from a single piece of cloth. Tunics were knee-length for working people or slaves, and ankle-length for wealthier citizens. The classic dress for women was a peplos – a sleeveless tunic with a high belt. It was pinned at each shoulder. Various styles of chiton also came into fashion. These were lighter, looser tunics, often with sleeves. Men also wore a simple version of the chiton.

necklace
c. 450BCE

To keep cool, the himation is draped low.

earrings
c. 850BCE

gold ring
c. 450BCE

MENSWEAR

This man wears no under-tunic or chiton, just a large wrap or himation. This was much like the toga worn by Roman men. Men would often wear no clothes at all for exercise, athletics or military training.

GLEAMING GOLD

Gold, silver, ivory and precious stones were made into beautiful earrings, headdresses, pendants, necklaces and rings. These were often costly gifts and brought out only on special occasions. Rings were sometimes worn as lucky charms or in honour of the gods.

 www.metmuseum.org/toah/hd/grd/hd_grdr.htm

⊖ OUT AND ABOUT

Greeks often went barefoot, especially in the home. The normal footwear was a pair of sandals made of leather thongs. Short or high boots could be worn for riding or working outdoors. During hot Mediterranean summers, a broad, brimmed straw hat was ideal. On cooler, more wintry days, a cap or a fur hat might be needed, as well as a warm, woollen cloak.

brimmed hat

leather sandal   high boot

MARBLE – a type of rock, often white in colour, used to make statues and buildings

CARVED COLUMNS

The Greeks were masters of arts and crafts, producing objects with technical skill and a sense of beauty. Magnificent public buildings and temples were supported by tall pillars, designed in various styles called 'orders'. Their tops, or capitals, were beautifully carved. Greek architecture, with its perfect proportions, would be imitated for thousands of years.

capital

pillar

Doric
fluted (lined) column with a plain, simple capital

Ionic
capital (top) is carved with a graceful scroll

CREATING BEAUTY

Greek cities were noisy, industrious places. Around the agora, the central market, were busy workshops where smiths hammered iron and bronze, silversmiths made jewellery and stone workers chiselled blocks of marble. Potters produced fine vases, decorated at first with geometric patterns and later with figures of people or gods in black and red. Some goods were made on a large scale and exported around the Mediterranean.

⊜ THE POTTER'S CRAFT

Many Greek city-states had access to good clay. This sticky mud was used to make urns, vases, dishes, jugs and jars. These were generally shaped on a potter's wheel and fired (baked) in a kiln until hard. During the firing, the amount of air could be varied, which made the clay turn red. Areas painted with a coating, called a slip, remained black.

Geometrical ware
patterned jug with a decorative spout, c. 675–650BCE

Red figure ware
shows a scene from the Trojan War, c. 480BCE

Black figure ware
cup featuring a bird-catcher from Etruria (an area of central Italy), c. 550BCE

> Archaeologists have discovered that many marble statues were originally coloured with paints.

www.schoolsliaison.org.uk/kids/greecepot.htm

Corinthian
*slender column
is topped with ornate
stone leaves*

**Statues of women, called
caryatids, served as
pillars at the front of
some buildings.**

LIVING MARBLE

Greek sculptors worked in marble, bronze and clay.
The first statues looked rather stiff and unnatural.
After the 500s CE, the human body was shown in a
much more realistic way for the first time in history.

HOT METAL

Blacksmiths used furnaces to heat iron. They raised
the heat by puffing in air, using leather bellows. They
shaped the soft metal into tools and weapons. Other
specialists worked precious ornamental metals such as
gold, silver and electrum (a mixture of the two metals).

"BEAUTY IS TRUTH, TRUTH BEAUTY."
John Keats (1795–1821)
English poet, from his poem Ode on a Grecian Urn *(1819)*

THE OLYMPIC GAMES

"LIVE BY RULE, SUBMIT TO DIET...
EXERCISE YOUR BODY AT STATED
HOURS, IN HEAT OR IN COLD..."

Epictetus (55–135CE)
philosopher, his words on training for the Olympics,
from The Enchiridion (135CE)

PENTATHLON – a five-event athletic contest

Thrilling athletic contests, or games, were held in Delphi, Nemea, Corinth and Olympia that were open to athletes from all over the Greek world. The games began as a kind of religious festival, held in honour of the gods. The Olympic Games are believed to have started in 776BCE and were celebrated every four years until 393CE. They were revived as an international competition in 1896 and have become the biggest sporting event of the modern world.

statue of Zeus as Horkios, taker of oaths, with a lightning bolt in each hand

RUNNING FOR ZEUS

During the Olympic Games, city-states had to stop fighting one another. Nobody travelling to the games could be harmed, for they were under the special protection of the gods. Athletes and officials joined a two-day procession from Elis to Olympia – a valley in the south-west of Greece – where there was a great temple dedicated to Zeus. There they were welcomed by an excited crowd. The Olympic site included other temples, tracks, racecourses, hostels and restaurants.

TOP EVENTS

The footrace was originally the most important event in the games. The first known Olympic champion was Coroebus, a baker from Elis, in 776BCE. Javelin, discus (left), running and long jump were not separate events, but part of the pentathlon, which was decided by a wrestling match between the top two athletes.

Boars are sacrificed to Zeus, king of the gods.

> Women held their own separate games at Olympia, in honour of the goddess Hera (see page 14).

www.olympic.org/ancient-olympic-games

THRILLS AND SPILLS

More sports were added to the games, including boxing, running in armour, all-in combat and horseracing. One of the most popular events was chariot racing, with teams of two or four horses. The action was fast and furious, and very dangerous for the charioteer.

The games begin with a swearing-in ceremony at the council chamber.

THE CHAMPIONS

At the end of the games, the winners were summoned to the Temple of Zeus. They were not given medals, but were crowned by the judges with a wreath of olive leaves. Finally, a great feast was held in their honour.

FAIR PLAY

Athletes were not supposed to be paid, but a winner could expect to be showered with gifts when he returned to his home city. Sometimes, there were political rows and accusations of foul play. Fines imposed on cheats were used to pay for new statues of Zeus at Olympia.

Athletes, holding portions of the sacrifice, swear to obey the rules.

Athletes, their families and trainers, and Olympic officials all queue to take the oath to Zeus.

MASKS AND MUSIC

The Greeks loved words and the sound of words – poetry, music and performing arts, such as dance and theatre. All these activities were closely linked and were said to be inspired by divine spirits called the Muses. The arts were powerfully connected with ancient religious rituals and festivals, but they were also rooted in the everyday life of village and town, and in fun and entertainment.

▽ LYRE – a stringed musical instrument, originally with a tortoiseshell sound-box

THE POET
Homer's poetry described wars and adventures. Later poets were more personal – praising nature or love, or grieving for the dead. Poetry accompanied by the music of a lyre was called 'lyric'. One popular lyric poet was Sappho (above) from Lesbos.

THE DANCERS
Frenzied dancing was part of the worship of Dionysus, while stately dances to a lyre's music honoured the god Apollo. There were dances for war, weddings, funerals and entertainment.

theatron – where the audience sit to view the performance

Theatres are semi-circular, with raised rows of stone benches.

TRAGEDY OR COMEDY?
Greek drama began as religious ritual and was a powerful creative force that soon took on a wider role in society. Greek dramatists of the 500s and 400s BCE, such as Aeschylus, Sophocles, Euripides and Aristophanes, shaped our modern ideas of theatre. They wrote sad, serious plays called tragedies, as well as funny plays called comedies. Actors performed by daylight in the open air, with seats in raised rows on which the audience watched the action on the stage.

THE CHORUS
In front of the stage, at least a dozen performers represented a group of characters – such as the women of a city – and sang or chanted together in verse. The chorus commented on the characters or explained the action of the play.

> Theatre masks had funnel-shaped mouths that may have been used to amplify the voice (make it louder).

"OH THEBES... OH CITY...
COME DANCE THE
DANCE OF GOD!"

Euripides (c. 480–406BCE)
spoken by the chorus in his play Bacchae *(405BCE)*

*An actor playing a
god is lowered by
a crane and cable.*

MASKS

Actors wore exaggerated
masks to make them appear
larger than life. They showed
a character's age, sex and
mood, and made it easier
for one actor to play several
roles. Both male and female
parts were played by men.

⊖ MAKER OF SWEET MUSIC

Myths tell of a musician called
Orpheus, whose playing of the
lyre calmed wild beasts and
brought nature to a standstill.
People played music when
going into battle, at sporting
events, in religious processions
and for private entertainment.
Instruments included the lyre
and *kithara*, as well as trumpets,
cymbals, flutes, double pipes or
auloi, pipes of Pan and drums.

Orpheus playing his lyre

www.bbc.co.uk/schools/primaryhistory/ancient_greeks/arts_and_theatre

*The main action
of a tragedy is
staged here.*

*Slain heroes
are rolled on
to the stage.*

**skene – the building
behind the stage in
which the costumes
were stored**

*Costumes are
richly detailed and
brightly coloured.*

*An altar to the god
Dionysus stands
in the orchestra.*

*The most important
people sit in the
front row.*

*Audiences
can number
15,000 or more.*

**orchestra – the
central area where
the chorus performs**

"EUREKA!"

"I've got it!" The story is told that these words were spoken by the scientist Archimedes, when he solved a problem of physics while taking a bath. He was born in the Greek colony of Syracuse, in Sicily, in about 287BCE. He was a great mathematician and physicist, who was famous for his useful inventions. Archimedes was killed during a Roman attack on Syracuse in about 212BCE.

Archimedes' screw

The rotating blades of the screw could raise water from one place to another.

This bronze calculator was found in a shipwreck. It contains more than 30 miniature gears.

Antikythera mechanism

ENQUIRING MINDS

The ancient Greeks believed in using human wisdom to solve their problems. They encouraged calm, sensible discussions about society and politics, and discovered science, mathematics, astronomy, geography and the world of nature. They were interested in medicine and technology. Greek thinkers, or philosophers, changed the way in which we see the world. Their ideas took root far beyond Europe and still influence us today.

SPACE AND PLANETS

Could this be the first computer? The Antikythera mechanism was used for precise astronomical calculations about 2,150 years ago. By about 260BCE, Aristarchus of Samos had even worked out that Earth and the planets move around the sun.

> Eratosthenes (276–195BCE) may have estimated the distance around the Earth to within one per cent of the correct figure.

Pythagoras' theorem
$$a^2 + b^2 = c^2$$

WORKING IT OUT

The Greeks loved puzzling over problems such as geometry – the mathematics of lines, angles and areas. In school, we still learn about the area of squares around a right-angled triangle, a problem associated with Pythagoras (c. 570–495BCE). The greatest master of geometry was a genius called Euclid, who lived in about 300BCE.

BRAINSTORMERS

Aristotle

Philosophy means the 'love of wisdom'. Greek philosophers liked to argue about the natural world, or how society should be organized. They asked questions about human behaviour and what is right and wrong. Aristotle (384–322BCE) was one of the first great scientists. Socrates (c. 469–399BCE) was a philosopher who was put to death for spreading dangerous political ideas. Plato (c. 428–348BCE) founded the Academy in Athens, a centre of philosophical debate.

www.ancientgreece.co.uk/knowledge/explore/exp_set.html

healing a patient who has suffered a snake bite

GREEK MEDICINE

Herbal cures and surgery took place at the shrines of Asclepius, the god of healing. Hippocrates of Kos (c. 460–370BCE) called for careful observation of patients and the study of their symptoms. Greek ideas about medicine were accepted in Europe and western Asia until the 1600s.

THE WIDER WORLD

As Greek sailors set out in search of new lands, geographers tried to make sense of the known world. The first one to try to draw a world map, with Greece at the centre, was probably Anaximander (c. 610–546BCE). This map is based on the ideas of Hecataeus (550–476BCE).

PHALANX – a battle formation perfected by the Macedonians

THE MARCH INTO ASIA

In 334BCE, Alexander crossed into Asia with an army of 30,000 foot soldiers and 5,000 cavalry. Ahead lay the troops of Darius III, emperor of Persia. Alexander's men fought their way across Asia Minor and conquered the lands known today as Syria, Lebanon, Egypt, Iraq, Iran, parts of Central Asia and Afghanistan. Darius suffered bitter defeats at the Granicus river, at Issus and Gaugamela. Alexander was victorious.

"O MY SON... MACEDONIA IS TOO SMALL FOR YOU."

King Philip II (382–336BCE)
said to his young son Alexander, as reported by the Greek historian Plutarch (c. 46–120CE)

ALEXANDER THE GREAT

King Alexander III was born in Pella, Macedonia, in 356BCE. As a boy, his tutor was the great philosopher Aristotle. In his short life, Alexander ('the Great') proved himself to be a brilliant general. He conquered one of the greatest empires the world had ever seen.

INDIAN WARFARE

In 326BCE, Alexander reached the Hydaspes river – known today as the Jhelum, in Pakistan. He defeated an Indian army under King Puravura, who had 200 war elephants in his army.

THE AGE OF ALEXANDER

Macedonia was a kingdom on the northern borders of Greece. It became very powerful under the rule of a king called Philip II. In 338BCE, Philip defeated an alliance of city-states, including Athens and Thebes, at the battle of Chaeronea. He was murdered two years later. His son Alexander became king. Alexander put down rebellions and planned a war of all the Greeks against the old enemy, Persia.

DARIUS AT ISSUS

This mosaic picture, made in Italy in about 100BCE, shows Alexander (below, left) fighting Darius (below), probably at the battle of Issus in 333BCE. Darius was killed by his own men in 330BCE. Alexander gave him a fine funeral.

DEATH IN BABYLON

By 323BCE, Alexander was in Babylon, in what is now Iraq. After a feast in the royal palace, he suffered a severe fever. Some people believed he had caught a disease, such as malaria. Others thought he was poisoned by jealous rivals. He died aged only 32.

coins from the time of Alexander the Great

www.historyofmacedonia.org/AncientMacedonia/AlexandertheGreat.html

☻ THE FEARSOME PHALANX

The phalanx was a terrifying battle formation made up of a great block of fighting men with spears. The Spartans used short spears, but the Macedonians used huge spears called sarissas that were up to 6.5m long. The front ranks pointed them forwards. The rear held them up at angles to break the flights of arrows.

Macedonian phalanx in battle order

GREATER GREECE

HELLENISTIC - following the Greek way from 323 to 30BCE

After the death of Alexander in 323BCE, the huge empire was fought over by his generals, who were hungry for power. In the end, it broke up into separate, Greek-ruled kingdoms – Macedonia-Greece, Egypt, the Seleucid empire (across the Middle East) and Pergamon in Asia Minor. These were stormy times, but the Greek way of life spread far and wide. This is known as the Hellenistic period of Greek history.

A Roman army uses elephants to scatter the Macedonian phalanx at the battle of Cynoscephalae, in Thessaly, in 197BCE.

The war elephants are armoured, with metal tips on their tusks.

Elephants were widely used in warfare – they were the ancient equivalent of tanks.

The last Greek ruler of Egypt was a famous queen called Cleopatra, who died in 30BCE.

GREEKS AND ASIANS

This stone carving in the Greek style belonged to a Buddhist monument from Gandhara, a kingdom in what is now Afghanistan and Pakistan. For centuries, Greek and Asian art and thought influenced each other in this region.

THE WELL-PLANNED CITY

Fine new cities were planned and built across the Hellenistic world, decorated with highly realistic statues. Priene, on the coast of Asia Minor, was rebuilt to a regular grid pattern, with well-drained streets, magnificent temples, public buildings, a theatre and a sports stadium.

GREECE VERSUS ROME

In the 300s and 200s BCE, the Italian city of Rome became ever more powerful. It conquered the Greek colonies in Italy and its armies soon marched into North Africa and western Asia. Macedonia was finally defeated in 168BCE after many battles, such as Cynoscephalae. After the Achaean War of 147–146BCE, all Greece came under Roman rule. The Greeks had lost their freedom – but their ways of life inspired the Romans as they in their turn built cities and a great empire.

www.livius.org/ct-cz/cynoscephalae/cynoscephalae.html

A BEACON IN THE NIGHT

This tall lighthouse was built in about 267BCE in Greek-ruled Egypt. It was sited at the port of Alexandria, which was named after Alexander the Great. The city became a major centre of learning and was famous for its great library.

LEGACY – something that is handed on to future generations

GREEK LEGACY

Many different lands shaped the civilizations of ancient Greece, from Europe to western Asia and Egypt. Classical Greece provided the foundations for a new European culture, with its great achievements in philosophy, politics, mathematics, architecture, drama and music. Even today, European languages are full of words that come from ancient Greek. Ideas from that distant period of history have spread around the modern world.

GREEKS AND ROMANS

The first part of this memorial is written in the Greek language and letters. The second part is in Latin, the language of Rome. Many Romans could speak Greek, and the two Mediterranean peoples shared similar beliefs and customs.

THE BYZANTINES

In 667BCE, the Greeks founded a colony named Byzantium. In 330CE, the Romans built a fine new city on the site, calling it Constantinople (now named Istanbul). It became the eastern capital of the Roman empire, thriving long after Rome had lost power, and became the centre of a Christian 'Byzantine' empire. Constantinople was captured by Muslim Turks in 1453. Greece won independence from Turkish rule in 1832.

Hagia Sophia, Istanbul

The splendid Christian Church of Holy Wisdom was completed in 537CE. It later became a Muslim mosque and it has been a museum since 1935.

> The modern Greek language is spoken by about 11 million people in Greece and by a further two million worldwide.

⊖ THE GREAT REVIVAL

Many ancient Greek ideas were respected by Christians in the Middle Ages. Precious records of their work were protected by scholars in the Muslim world. In the 1400s and 1500s, there was a great revival or 'Renaissance' of interest in ancient Greece and Rome. Greek and Latin were taught in schools. Discoveries of sites such as Mycenae and Knossos fascinated new generations in the 1800s and 1900s.

http://byzantium.seashell.net.nz/articlemain.php?artid-mapbase_565

Plato and Aristotle feature in this 1510–11 painting by Raphael, an artist of the Italian Renaissance.

JUSTINIAN THE GREAT

Justinian I was emperor from 527 to 565CE. He set about winning back the lands of the western Roman empire. In his own eastern empire, Roman law was still used, but people spoke Greek and its 'Orthodox' forms of Christian worship developed separately from those of Rome.

The minarets (prayer towers) date from the building's period as a Turkish mosque.

DEMOKRATÍA

The modern Greek parliament meets in Athens, where the idea of democracy was born more than 2,500 years ago. Modern governments may view democracy in many different ways, but most still claim that rule by the people is central to their ideals as a nation.

GLOSSARY

AGORA
The central market and business district in a Greek town; the forum.

ALL-IN COMBAT
Fighting, wrestling and boxing at the same time.

ALTAR
A table or slab where offerings are made to a god or goddess.

ARCHAEOLOGIST
Someone who looks for ancient sites, making a methodical, scientific study of remains and ruins.

BRAZIER
A moveable metal container for holding charcoal or burning wood.

BRONZE
A metal that is an alloy (mixture) of copper and tin, and used for making tools and weapons.

CHARIOT
A light cart, normally pulled by horses, used in warfare or sport.

CHORUS
A group of men who performed identical actions and speech during a theatrical performance.

CITY-STATE
A small, independent nation based on a single city and the surrounding region or island.

CONQUER
To defeat an enemy, often invading their lands.

DEMOCRACY
Rule by the people, or by their representatives.

EMPIRE
A number of different lands coming under a single ruler.

EPIC
A long and exciting story about heroic adventures.

FORTIFICATION
Walls, ditches, towers or forts built for defence or attack.

GRID PATTERN
A town plan that has straight roads crossing each other at regular intervals.

HELMSMAN
The person who steers a boat or ship.

HIMATION
A large, loose cloak worn by both men and women in ancient Greece.

HOPLITE
An ancient Greek footsoldier armed with a spear, sword and shield.

IMMORTAL
Someone who lives for ever. A member of the Persian royal guard was called an Immortal because whenever one was killed in battle, another immediately took his place.

KILN
A very hot oven used to 'fire' (bake and harden) pottery.

LOOM
A frame used for weaving cloth.

MINOAN

Belonging to the first great civilization on the island of Crete, from about 2700 to 1420BCE.

MINT

1) To make metal coins; 2) the place where coins are made.

MOSAIC

A picture made from many small, coloured tiles or fragments of pottery, stone or glass.

MUSES

Nine goddesses or spirits believed to inspire activities such as music, dance, poetry or drama. The words 'music' and 'museum' come from the word *mousieon*, a shrine to the muses.

MYCENAEAN

Belonging to the civilization that grew around the citadels of southern Greece, from about 1600 to 1100BCE.

OFFERING

A sacrifice or gift offered to a god or goddess, perhaps at a shrine or an altar.

ORCHESTRA

A performance space in front of the main stage used by the chorus in an ancient Greek theatre.

ORTHODOX

Following a correct or traditional form of worship – as practised, for example, by the Greek Orthodox Church.

POLITICS

The study or practice of government or ways of bringing about social change.

RITUAL

A ceremony or series of acts used in religion and worship.

SACRIFICE

A gift to a god or goddess. In ancient Greece it was usually an animal, such as a white bull, killed at an altar.

SARISSA

A very long spear used by a Macedonian phalanx in battle.

SCRIPT

A form of writing, such as an alphabet.

SHRINE

A holy place or a temple.

SLAVE

Someone who has no freedom, and who is bought, sold and forced to work for no reward.

STATESMAN

A leading politician.

STERN

The back end of a boat or ship.

TRIDENT

A three-pronged spear. It is a symbol of the god Poseidon.

TRIREME

A warship with three banks of rowers.

WARE

A type or style of pottery.

YARN

Thread that has been spun from a loose fibre, such as wool. Women wove yarn into cloth for clothing, using large looms.

INDEX

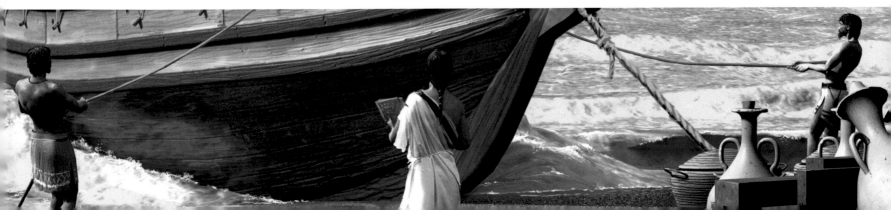

INVESTIGATE

The world of ancient Greece may not be as far away as you think – just look in a museum, in a book, or on the stage or screen.

MUSEUMS AND EXHIBITIONS

In most countries in Europe and in many British cities you will find museums showing beautiful Greek pottery, statues, coins or jewellery.

📖 *The Pocket Timeline of Ancient Greece* by Emma McAllister (British Museum Press)

✦ Ashmolean Museum of Art and Archaeology, Beaumont Street, Oxford, OX1 2PH, UK

🌐 www.ashmolean.org

clay tablet showing a woman at a table from Locris, Greece

ruins of the Temple of Poseidon, Sounion, Greece

ARCHAEOLOGY

If you are interested in archaeology, make a start by joining a local group for young people. If you go on holiday to Greece, Turkey or southern Italy, you can even visit the ancient Greek sites for yourself.

📖 *Greece* by Stephen Biesty (Oxford University Press)

✦ Palace of Knossos, near Heraklion, Crete

🌐 www.ancient-greece.org/archaeology.html

scene from a film about Alexander the Great

FICTION, STAGE AND SCREEN

Myths, legends and tales of ancient Greece have always inspired writers and film-makers, and they can recreate the ancient magic just for you. Why not make Greek masks or put on a Greek drama at your school?

writings of the ancient Greek historian Herodotus can be read today

📖 *Black Ships Before Troy* by Rosemary Sutcliffe (Frances Lincoln)

✦ *Hercules* DVD (Walt Disney Home Video)

🌐 www.greektheatre.gr

RESEARCH

A visit to your local library is sure to offer information on ancient Greece. To see hoplites in action, check out re-enactment performances near you.

📖 *The Usborne Encyclopedia of Ancient Greece* by Jane Chisholm (Usborne)

✦ British Museum, Great Russell Street, London, WC1B 3DG, UK

🌐 www.hoplites.org/index.htm